T0381045

1000 Faces of Grief

By Bill Griffin

Copyright © 2019 Bill Griffin.

All rights reserved. No part of this book may be used or reproduced by any means, graphic, electronic, or mechanical, including photocopying, recording, taping or by any information storage retrieval system without the written permission of the author except in the case of brief quotations embodied in critical articles and reviews.

This book is a work of non-fiction. Unless otherwise noted, the author and the publisher make no explicit guarantees as to the accuracy of the information contained in this book and in some cases, names of people and places have been altered to protect their privacy.

Balboa Press books may be ordered through booksellers or by contacting:

Balboa Press
A Division of Hay House
1663 Liberty Drive
Bloomington, IN 47403
www.balboapress.com
1 (877) 407-4847

Because of the dynamic nature of the Internet, any web addresses or links contained in this book may have changed since publication and may no longer be valid. The views expressed in this work are solely those of the author and do not necessarily reflect the views of the publisher, and the publisher hereby disclaims any responsibility for them.

Interior Image Credit: Marcus Schneider

ISBN: 978-1-9822-3328-0 (sc)
ISBN: 978-1-9822-3329-7 (e)

Library of Congress Control Number: 2019912167

Print information available on the last page.

Balboa Press rev. date: 08/28/2019

BALBOA
PRESS
A DIVISION OF HAY HOUSE

This book is dedicated to my wife, Mary Catherine

Acknowledgements

A huge and humble thanks to the "Experts". These are the people that shared their experiences in the Grief Support Groups.

A special thanks to my wife, Mary Catherine and my daughter, Debbie, for their guidance and editing skills.

With his photographic skills and his exceptional support, Marcus Schneider brought the photos to life.

Table of Contents

Introduction

If you have lost a loved one, then you have met the Faces of Grief, but may not have recognized them. They are responsible for the intense pain and tears that come unexpectedly. Find out who these Faces are and how they create such pain.

Is it possible to heal from losing your spouse, child, parent, or a brother or sister? Only you know the depth of your love and grief. Whether you are just starting your journey of grief or have been on it for a long time, let your heart respond to the photos, jigsaw puzzle and Grief-O-Meter. Tears, smiles, deep sadness and gratitude may all occur. Accept where you are at right now.

You are going to be okay and this book will help you get there, because it lets you decide what works best for you.

Who are the Faces of Grief

Many people have experienced Grief, but may not have recognized the Faces. Grief is a 1000 faces in a 1000 places waiting to jab you right in your heart. They lurk in the night and the day, at home, in the car and unexpected places and times.

Grief is often described by the emotions (words) it causes. But these are not just words. The Faces of Grief each have the name of an emotion and have a very real impact on your life.

Only you know which Faces are causing you the most pain. Some of the names of these Faces are:

Loss	Holidays
Loneliness	Overwhelming
Financial worries	Daily chores
Denial	Guilt
Emptiness	Anger
Sleeplessness	Left out
Anxiety	Why
Helplessness	Social situations

Turn the page and look at the Faces. Do certain Faces draw your attention? What name would you assign to those Faces?

To see how these Faces have impacted your life, go to the page "What Happened".

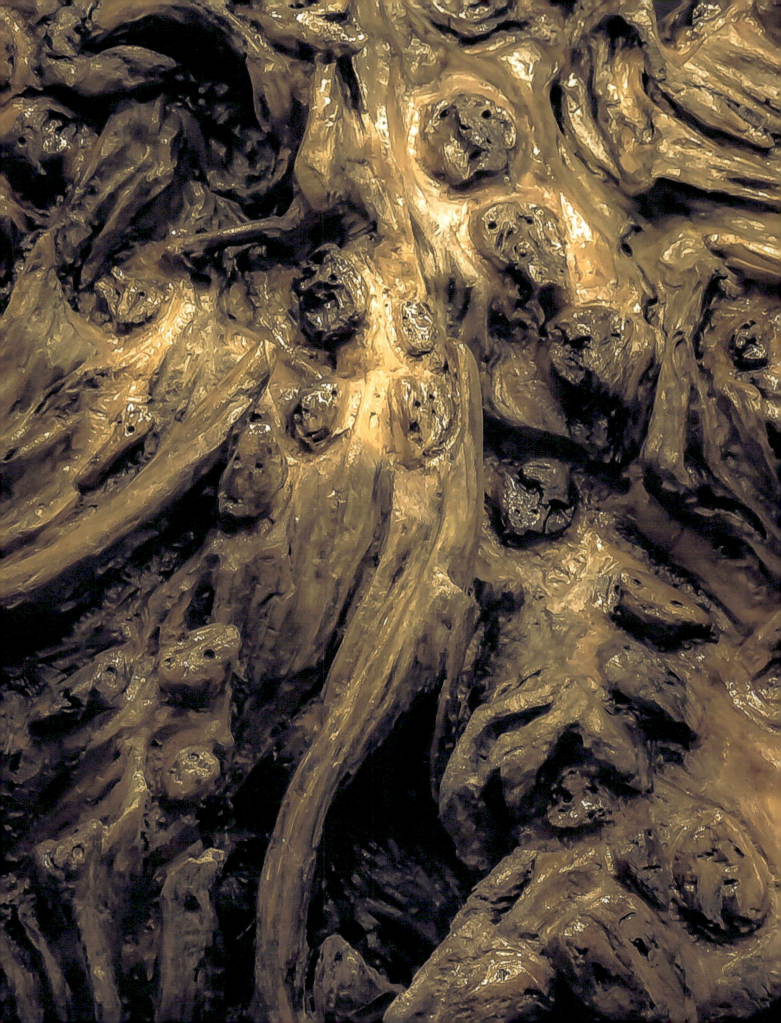

What Happened?

Writing answers to these questions will help you understand what is happening to your life. Mark the date you do this, because you may want to come back in six months, a year or sometime later and fill it out again.

The Faces of Grief have created a new life for you that you never asked for.

Has the death of your loved one:

	Yes	No	How
Changed the way you eat			
Changed the way you watch TV			
Changed your circle of friends			
Changed your family dynamics			
Changed your self-confidence			
Caused brain fog			
Changed your sense of security			
Changed your interests			
Changed how you spend your time			
Changed how you respond to people's comments			
Changed how you celebrate			

Chapter 1

ALONE NOW

It starts the moment your loved one leaves this earth. The Faces of Grief are anxious to be your constant companions. Loneliness is so consuming. Will each day be better or worse?

Is the little boy burying something? That is a very big beach. Where are all the other people?

Photos relating to the loss of a spouse, child, parent, sibling or a caregiver are on the following pages. The Faces of Grief use all kinds of things to torment you and remind you of your loss. Let the photos guide your feelings. Let the tears come and wash away some of the pain in your heart.

Losing your Spouse

The Faces of Grief want to interrupt your everyday life and use common things to trigger that pain. Let the photos speak to you and write whatever you want beside them. If you are not ready today, come back tomorrow or another day.

Losing your child

To Monica
By Mary Leal

I used to see you in the crib
    smiling up at me.
I saw you toddle through the yard
    and try to climb a tree.

I watched you learn so many things
    through your years in school.
You learned to play piano
    and grew to love the pool.

I saw you with your babies
    I watched you watch them grow
I lost sight of you along the way
    Why I don't know.

the rest of the "To Monica" poem
is on page 13

Can you smell the chocolate chip cookies baking?

Who is going to tell the recipe book that Mom will not be using it again?

Did your Dad fix your broken bike?

The tie is wondering why it has been
Left in the closet?

People said it was easy to tell we were related.

Our rock seems so big and empty now.

Being the Caregiver

The doctor's assessment was like a storm that shoved your ship crashing into a large rock. The damage could not be fixed.

Each day the ship would sink a bit further.

Frustration.   Helplessness.

Here, take some more medicine.

The last sail has disappeared under the water.

Relief?   Guilt?

Chapter 2

HEALING

Healing

Healing – what does that really mean? The bouquet can never be put back together into its original beauty.

Is it possible to get relief from the intense pain caused by the Faces of Grief? The poem "Special Person" on the next page calls your loved one a gift to you. Read it slowly and relive the intensity of your love and the wonderful impact your loved one had on your life.

As you look at the photos on the following pages, let your heart respond to whatever emotions are happening right now. Do not judge yourself or let others advise you to get on with your life.

If the Face of Guilt is still clinging to your legs, consider doing the suggestions in the section on Guilt. You may be surprised how effective they can be in helping you get through this part of grieving.

There is still a jigsaw puzzle and a Grief-O-Meter ahead as you go through the rest of the book to the important last page.

Special Person

God said "Would you like to have a very special person in your life?
And He gave me you.

Being with you was a miracle that dwells in the heart.

In the quiet of the night, I hear you softly calling my name, and it
makes my spirits soar like a seagull on the ocean breeze.

There were times we laughed and times when we cried.

There were times when life was crazy and times when it was so quiet and peaceful.

When you were called home by God, it felt like a cold,
driving rain engulfed me and it would never let up.

Now with time and your presence, I can touch your
picture and our memories and feel your love.

Push apart the clouds so I can see the blue sky – where you live with God.

In Gratitude for Your Spouse

Remember our first secret kiss?

So much love and so much loss.
(Add your words, feelings, pain)

In Gratitude for Your Child

Yesterday

You watched your child travel further each day, but they still wanted that goodnight hug.

Today and Tomorrow

So now I'll see you in the stars and in the moon and sun. View you in the summer flowers and miss you when they are gone.

But someday soon we'll meet again with dancing and guitars. We'll share a smile, but until then I'll see you in the stars.

(This is the rest of the poem "To Monica, by Mary Leal. The first part is on page 4)

In Gratitude for Your Mother

All Moms gave the gift of love in one way or another. Yes, they saved your precious childhood artwork.

Fill out the lists below. The gifts you list cannot be put in a box with a ribbon on it

Gifts your Mother gave to you   **Gifts you gave to your Mother**

_____   _____

_____   _____

_____   _____

_____   _____

_____   _____

Did your Dad have a soft spot for the little guy?

Sometimes Dad did not know how to fix if for you and appeared not to care.
Some Dads hug from a distance.

If you could talk to your Dad or write him a letter, what would you say?

Secrets shared

Quiet companionship

The two plants give life and respect to our special rock. Each plant is different, yet similar, just like us. What stories would the rock tell about us if it could talk?

In Gratitude to the Caregiver

A Caregiver's Hands

Your hands reached out to hold their hand during the long nights.

Your hands reached out to wipe away a tear.

Your hands reached out to comfort them before another treatment.

Your hands reached out to offer your gifts of love and compassion.

Your hands reached out to open the blinds so they could marvel at the sunset.

Your hands reached out to bring them chocolate and flowers.

Your hands reached out to say "Goodbye" as the left this world.

In Gratitude for Your Loved One's Presence

Communication or feeling their presence can happen any time and anywhere.

When you feel you may be ready, going back to a favorite spot may be painful, but healing. Remember the picnic area that was kind of secluded around the bend in the river.

Does your picnic basket contain memories of hot dogs, laughter, bees, and smores?

How do you explain the rainbow ending right at your table? No, you are not weird or imagining things. It is a real rainbow just for you. Accept it with wonder and joy.

In Gratitude for

Candles

What happens if you light just one candle for yourself? Does the Face of Darkness laugh at you? Then find more candles and chase the Face into a corner. If you put the candles in front of a mirror, they reflect light back to you. Does this mean that you can give light to others and they will do the same for you? The more candles you light, the more reflection you see. Tears and hope and maybe a little bit of peace can share this moment.

Cemeteries

It is a place where you can visit your loved one and tell them about your pain and struggles. Others visiting the loved one will understand and may be willing to share their journey with you. If the cemetery seems like a cold place, then there is no guilt in not going there.

Family and friends

Everyone needs to respect where each person is in their grief. At times, companionship and listeners are desperately needed. Other times, you may want privacy. Family and friends will need someone to listen to them also. It is like walking down the road with your arms around each other's shoulders.

Dogs and cats

Just accept their unconditional love.

Flowers

Every flower blossoms into new life to give beauty to the world. Yes, they need nourishing. Accept some nourishing and when the time is right, your bud will appear and begin to blossom.

In Gratitude for Your Life

Life is a puzzle that you put together piece by piece.

Write in each piece whatever you want. It could be a place, time, event, quiet moment, personal trait or any combination. The memories will fit together perfectly.

The piece on the bottom is the one you will add as you move on in your life. What that piece will be is entirely up to you. It is your piece and you get to decide.

Chapter 3

GUILTY

GUILTY

GUILTY

"Welcome to the Lagoon of Guilt"

Step in and join me, the Face of Guilt. I will envelope your legs in a cold, slimy grip. You pronounced yourself "Guilty", so you deserve to be miserable – or do you?

The next three pages offer ideas and suggestions for dealing with Guilt. These may help to get through this part of grief and get back to shore, because most of the cold, slimy grip will have disappeared.

Guilt

Check off and write the reasons you feel guilty. Doing this may be difficult, but it can be healing.

Not spending enough time with them _____

Feeling you should have done more _____

Feeling like you are free and can move on _____

Feeling too exhausted to listen to them _____

Your own reasons

_____

_____

_____

_____

Go to the next page. After reviewing that, you will probably want to come back to this page and change some things.

How to Confront Guilt

Three terms need to be defined:

Guilt –actions or inactions intended to hurt or harm the person

Regrets – "What if", "Should have", "Could have" This was hoping for a better situation and outcome. There was never any intent to hurt or harm.

Relief – feeling guilty because you no longer have the burden of care.

Fill out these two columns

Positive things you did for them	Negative things you did or failed to do for them
_____	
_____	_____
_____	
_____	_____
_____	
_____	_____
_____	
_____	_____
_____	
_____	_____

Now go back to the earlier page where you wrote reasons for guilt. Using the definitions above, do you need to modify some of the information from Guilt to Regrets?

Guilt

Is the Face of Guilt still clinging to your legs?

Here is a way to make guilt disappear.

Write in ink on a white piece of paper all those reasons for guilt. Put that paper into a container of Chlorox. Check it a week later. The paper is blank and probably falling apart. All those reasons you wrote are gone. Who erased them- your loved one? God? Does it matter?

You have been forgiven.

Let the sun shine directly on you.

Chapter 4

NOW YOU ARE THE DRIVER

Driver

Now you are the driver. There are no direction or destination signs. You have a choice. You can either stay right here in the middle of the road or you can risk driving down that road. Those shadows across the road are the Faces of Fear, Self-confidence and Anxiety all telling you to stay and not go down there.

You had the courage to drive down the road, which ended in a gravel parking lot. A path leads down to the beach. Have you ever seen a beach with this many footprints, but not a single person in sight?

Is it possible that these are the footprints of all the people walking their journey of grief? Where are they all going? There does not seem to be a destination. Why is it so lonely? Aren't you supposed to get support from them?

As you walk down the beach, you come upon this little boy all by himself.

He looks up at you and asks if you will help him dig a big hole, so he can bury his sadness, and you can put yours in the hole too. Will you help him?

Now he wants to build a sandcastle on top of the hole. He explains how to build it, but you can do some of it your way. You probably have built sandcastles before, but none like this one. This one is suggesting you can rebuild your life. You can remember how to laugh and play. You can help others build their sandcastle and they will help you build yours. You were smart to lock the Faces of Grief in the car and not let them come with you to the beach.

The day is almost over and the sun is slipping below the horizon. As you walk with the little boy back to the parking area, you smile because your sandcastle is still standing strong against the threatening tide.

Face called Holidays

Back home, the Face of Grief called "Holidays" is waiting for you. With glee, it reminds you the first "Anniversary" is coming up next week. Has the tide washed away your sandcastle? Does anyone care? How can you get off this emotional roller coaster? Can you run and hide?

Friends are coming to support you on your "Anniversary". They will ask "How are you doing?". You will answer "Fine". They will say something about getting your life back together. Do you tell them the truth and make the conversation uncomfortable? Does anyone really want to hear about your pain and daily struggles? Love never dies and apparently the Faces of Grief never die either. You will be told it gets easier with time.

Tomorrow you can start the preparations for your "Anniversary" get-together.

Does the poem on the next page say what you are feeling?

Birthdays, Anniversaries, Holidays

You search for the perfect gift going store to store.

You pull out all the pots and pans to prepare that special meal.

You search for understanding as to what you are supposed to do.

You tried to put the Faces of Grief in the back bedroom and lock the door.

You search for peace or joy or a quiet heart or maybe just a hand to hold yours.

You search for strength as you open the door and greet those coming up the path

You try to be present and laugh at the appropriate times to show people you are okay.

You sit quietly after everyone has gone.

You give thanks for the hugs and unspoken compassion.

Tomorrow does not seem quite so challenging.

Chapter 5

THEIR THINGS

Does disposing of their things mean the love is also given away?

Giving away or disposing of their things does NOT mean giving away the love and memories associated with those things.

Some thoughts to consider

	Yes	No	Why
Is this the time to begin giving away their things?			_____
Do you feel guilty about giving their 'stuff" away?			_____
Ask family and/or friends to help?			_____
Listen to both your heart and your brain?			_____
Sort things into piles, such as "Keep", "Give away", "Maybe later?			_____
If most everything ends up in the pile "Keep", is that okay?			_____
Shut the closet door and try another day?			_____

GRIEF-O-METER

This is a scientific way to monitor your progress. Write the date and mark an "X" along the line. If the grouch on the end gets less and less "X's", you are winning the battle against the Faces of Grief.

Date

_____

_____

_____

_____

_____

_____

_____

_____

_____

Balancing My Life

Things change, yet they stay connected

Which words speak to you. You may want to do just a few words at a time and experience the feelings that occur. Your heart and mind will have suggestions for both sides. Also, add some of your own words in the middle column.

Connecting the memories with your life today shows you are going to be okay.

Memories		Today
_____	Flower	_____
_____	Ketchup	_____
_____	Pet peeve	_____
_____	Game	_____
_____	"Spilled milk"	_____
_____	Trips	_____
_____	Seasons	_____
_____	Vegetables	_____
_____	Helping others	_____

Chapter 6

LAST PAGE

But not the END

Last Page

Yes, this is the last page, but not the END

The yellow rose has been called the symbol of the soul.
Yellow is the light of the sun.
Green leaves represent new vibrant life.

You are my yellow rose that will never die,
because love is eternal
and not extinguished by death.

EPILOGUE

Keep on driving, marvel at the sunset
and make the Faces of Grief
always sit in the back seat.

Printed in the United States
By Bookmasters